DATE DUE

EASTERN
EUROPE

EASTERN EUROPE

country	area sq mi (sq km)	population (1996)	capital	currency
BULGARIA	42,823 (110,910)	8,415,000	Sofia	Lev
CZECH REPUBLIC	30,450 (78,864)	10,464,000	Prague	Koruna
HUNGARY	35,920 (93,030)	10,500,000	Budapest	Forint
POLAND	124,808 (312,680)	38,891,000	Warsaw	Zloty
ROMANIA	91,699 (237,500)	23,611,000	Bucharest	Leu
SLOVAKIA	18,933 (49,000)	5,381,000	Bratislava	Koruna

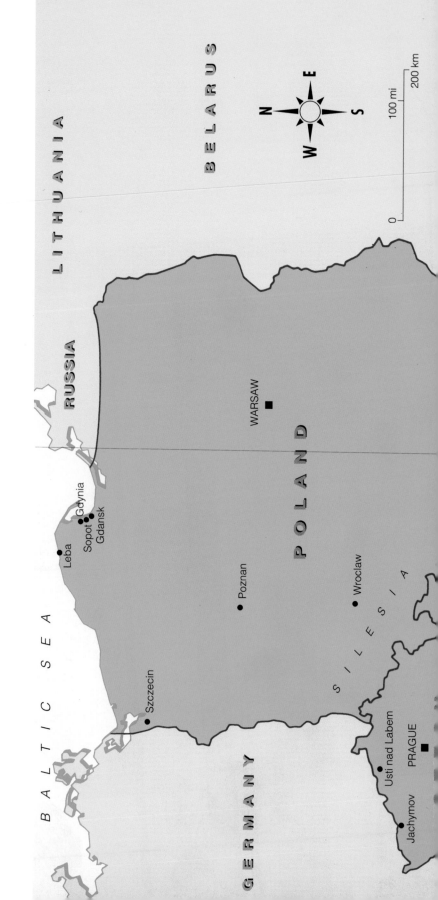

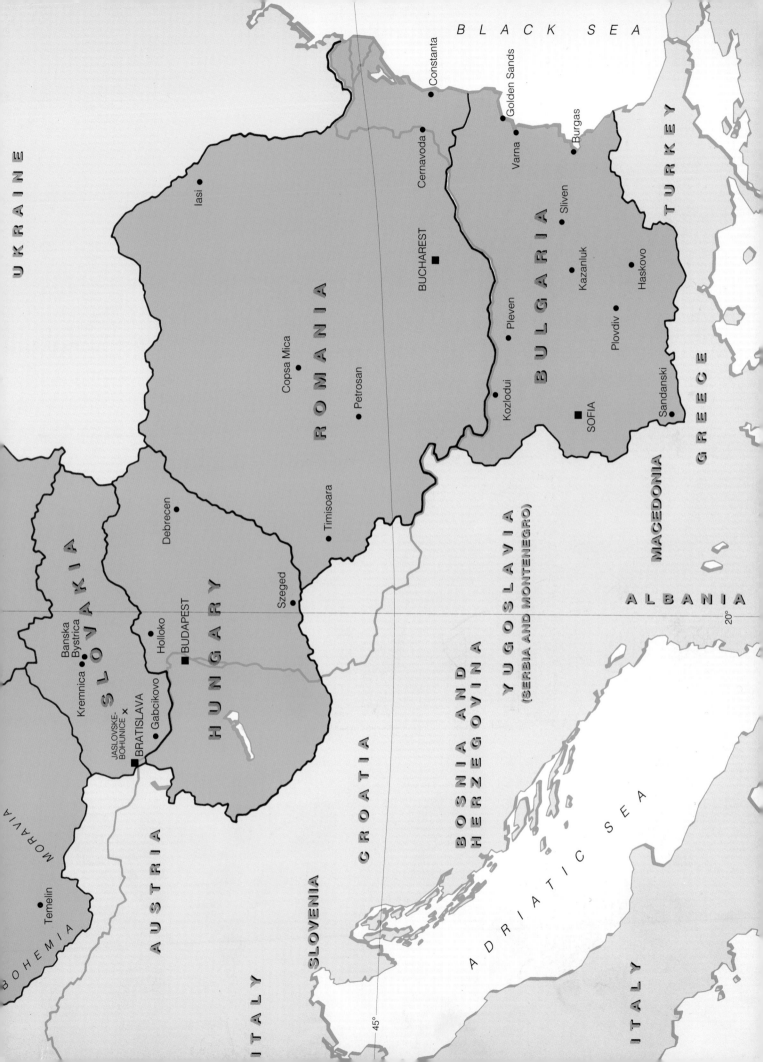

BULGARIA

CZECH REPUBLIC

HUNGARY

POLAND

ROMANIA

SLOVAKIA

EASTERN EUROPE

Patrick Burke

RSVP ®

**RAINTREE
STECK-VAUGHN**
P U B L I S H E R S
The Steck-Vaughn Company

Austin, Texas

Published by Raintree Steck-Vaughn Publishers, an imprint of Steck-Vaughn Company

Design and typesetting Roger Kohn Designs
Editors Diana Russell, Pam Wells
Picture research Valerie Mulcahy
Illustration János Márffy
Commissioning editor Debbie Fox

We are grateful to the following for permission to reproduce photographs:
Front Cover: Impact (Justin Williams) *above*; Tony Stone Images (Joe Cornish) *below*; Britstock IFA, page 11; Colorsport, page 25; Sue Cunningham, pages 32, 35, 36, 43, 44, 45; The Environmental Picture Library, pages 18 (Paul Glendell), 30 (Pilly Cowell); Robert Harding Picture Library, pages 31 (Loraine Wilson), 39 (Michael Short), 43 (Jan Baldwin); The Hutchinson Library, pages 19 (Carlos Freire), 25, 33 and 34 (Melanie Friend); Impact Photos, pages 15 (Peter Arkwell), 21 (John Cole), 29 (Simon Grosset); Magnum, pages 40 (Abbas), 41 (James Nachtwey); Panos Pictures, page 23 (Jeremy Hartley); Rex Features, pages 9 *right* (Andras Bankuti), 9 *left* Jon Player, 12 (Lasky), 16 (Sipa Press), 20, 40 (Richard Sowersby); Skoda, page 36; Spectrum Colour Library, page 13; Tony Stone Images, pages 8 (David Hanson), 20 (Zygmunt Nowak Solins), 38 (Gavin Hellier); Sygma, pages 14 (Alain Nogues), 26 (J. Langevin), 28 (Patrick Forestier), 29 (Thierry Orban), 42 (G. Giansanti); Topham Picturepoint, page 17; TRIP, pages 10 (W. Jacobs), 24 (J. Love), (F. Andreescu).

The statistics given in this book are the most up-to-date available at the time of going to press.

Printed in Hong Kong by Wing King Tong

2 3 4 5 6 7 8 9 0 HK 02 01 00 99 98

Library of Congress Cataloging-in-Publication Data
Burke, Patrick.
Eastern Europe / Patrick Burke
p. cm — (Country fact files)
Includes bibliographical references and index.
Summary: Looks at the geography, history, culture, and economy of Bulgaria, the Czech Republic, Hungary, Poland, Romania, and Slovakia.
ISBN 0-8172-4628-2
1. Europe, Eastern—Juvenile literature. [1. Europe, Eastern.]
I. Title. II. Series.
DJK39.5.B87 1997
947—dc21   96-35487
CIP
AC

CONTENTS

Words that are explained in the glossary are printed in SMALL CAPITALS the first time they are mentioned in the text.

INTRODUCTION

Eastern Europe includes the six countries of Bulgaria, the Czech Republic, Hungary, Poland, Romania, and Slovakia. The region's total population is 97,262,000. Its land area is 340,341 square miles (881,484 sq km), less than one-tenth the size of the United States.

Toward the end of World War II, in 1944–45, Eastern Europe was freed from the domination of Nazi Germany when the Soviet army moved in. The Soviet Union remained in control after the end of the war and imposed COMMUNISM on the region. For 40 years, Soviet-backed Communist regimes ruled over political systems in which no opposition parties were allowed to operate. Newspapers and broadcasting companies were controlled by the state, and most people were not allowed to travel abroad or could only do so with difficulty. In 1989, the Communist regimes were brought down, in popular revolutions

◀ *Since 1989, Prague has once again become an elegant city. The Old Town is one of the region's most popular tourist attractions and an important source of income for the Czech Republic.*

▶ *For this young couple in Bucharest, a horse-drawn cart is the only affordable form of transportation. Economic reforms have yet to improve the lives of many poorer Romanians.*

that were mostly peaceful. In Romania, however, the uprising cost the lives of 700 people, including those of the brutal dictator Nicolae Ceausescu and his wife, Elena, who were executed by a firing squad.

Today, all these states are in the middle of a slow and difficult period of change. Parliamentary DEMOCRACIES have been set up, and democratically elected governments are introducing Western-style MARKET ECONOMIES.

▶ **This giant statue of a worker once towered over a street in Budapest. Now Hungarian citizens can laugh at it—and 20 other Communist statues—in an outdoor museum on the edge of the city.**

● Population density: 42 per sq mi (108.9 per sq km), ranging from 30 in Bulgaria to 48 in Poland
● Capital cities: Bucharest, 2.07 million; Budapest, 2 million; Warsaw, 1.64 million; Prague, 1.21 million; Sofia, 1.11 million; Bratislava: 448,785
● Highest peak: Musala, Bulgaria 9,596 ft (2,925 m)
● Longest river: Danube, 1,777 mi (2,860 km) total, of which 994 mi (1,600 km) are in Eastern Europe
● Major languages: Polish, Romanian, Czech, Hungarian, Bulgarian, Slovak
● Major religions: Christianity (Roman Catholicism, Romanian Orthodox, Bulgarian Orthodox, Calvinist), Islam
● Major resources: Coal, natural gas, crude petroleum, copper, iron ore, salt
● Major products: Petroleum, natural gas, petroleum products, pig iron, steel, aluminum, cement, buses and cars, fertilizers, textiles and clothing, audio and electrical equipment
● Environmental problems: Industrial pollution (of air, soil, and water)

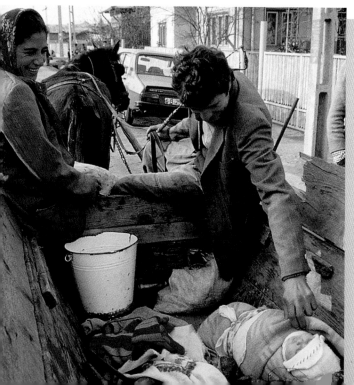

The economies of the Czech Republic, Slovakia, Poland, and Hungary are all growing. Signs of wealth, such as Western cars and stores and new construction, are visible in their capital cities, Prague, Bratislava, Warsaw, and Budapest. But the changes have also brought high unemployment—which officially did not exist under the old system—and new poverty. Meanwhile, the economies of Bulgaria and Romania in the southeast of the region—countries that are farther away from Western markets and less attractive to Western investors—are growing more slowly.

THE LANDSCAPE

Eastern Europe extends from the Polish Baltic Sea coast in the north to the Black Sea coastlines of Romania and Bulgaria in the southeast. Three countries—the Czech Republic, Slovakia, and Hungary—are landlocked. The region is bordered on the east by the states of the former Soviet Union; on the west by Germany, Austria, and the states of former Yugoslavia; and on the south by Greece and Turkey.

Eastern Europe's landscape varies from plains in Poland, Hungary, and on the border of Romania and Bulgaria, to the hills and mountains of the Czech Republic, Slovakia, Bulgaria, and Romania. Poland lies almost wholly on the Northern European Plain—more than 75 percent (%) of the country is less than 660 feet (200 m) above sea level—while the Great Plain of Hungary occupies more than half of that country's land area.

Between Poland and Hungary, Slovakia

▼ *A ski lodge and ski jump in the Czech Tatra Mountains. Skiers use many parts of the Carpathian range, where snow can lie on the higher peaks for up to 100 days a year.*

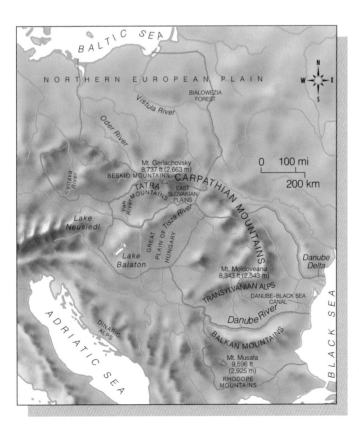

slopes down from the mountains in the north and center to the East Slovakian plains. The Czech Republic is almost entirely surrounded by hills and mountains.

The Carpathian range stretches in a huge arc from the Beskid and Tatra mountains on the borders of Poland, Slovakia, and the Czech Republic, down to the Transylvanian Alps. Its tallest peaks, in Slovakia and Romania, are more than 6,561 feet (2,000 m) high. About 60 percent of Bulgaria's land area consists of hills and mountains. The Balkan Mountains are in the center and the Rhodope Mountains are in the southwest.

At 1,777 miles (2,860 km), the Danube is Europe's second longest river, after the Volga. It rises in Germany, passes through Austria, and then flows through several other countries before it reaches Romania. Here, it empties into the Black Sea in three channels: the Chilia, the Sulina, and the Sfantu

Gheorghe. Between them lies the Danube DELTA, formed 6,000 years ago. The longest river that flows wholly through the region is Poland's Vistula, 675 miles (1,086 km).

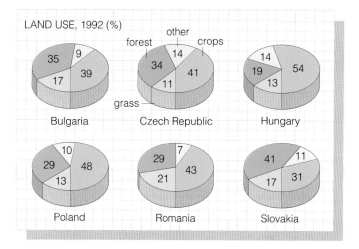

LAND USE, 1992 (%)

Bulgaria: 35, 9, 39, 17
Czech Republic: forest, other, crops, 34, 14, 41, 11, grass
Hungary: 14, 54, 13, 19
Poland: 10, 48, 13, 29
Romania: 7, 43, 21, 29
Slovakia: 41, 11, 31, 17

▼ *Over the centuries, the silt brought down the Danube has enlarged its delta into a network of channels, lakes, reed islands, pastures, woods, and sand dunes.*

CLIMATE AND WEATHER

Much of Eastern Europe has a transitional, or Central European, type of climate. It is called transitional because it shares the characteristics of two other climate types: maritime, to the west and north (including the United Kingdom and Ireland), where there is rain in all months and there are rarely great extremes of heat or cold; and continental, to the east (including Russia, eastern Belarus, and northern Ukraine), where there are warm summers and cold winters. However, within this pattern there are variations, which are

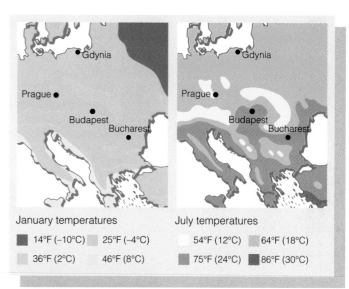

January temperatures

■ 14°F (–10°C)		□ 25°F (–4°C)	
□ 36°F (2°C)		□ 46°F (8°C)	

July temperatures

□ 54°F (12°C)		□ 64°F (18°C)	
□ 75°F (24°C)		■ 86°F (30°C)	

◀ *Winter in the Polish Tatras. The highest mountains are snowbound for most of the year. Houses are designed with sharply sloping roofs to minimize the amount of snow that settles on them.*

partly caused by differences in altitude.

In the north, on Poland's Baltic coast, winter is milder than in the east and south. Snow in the Tatra and Beskid mountains is heavy enough for winter sports. This is true of the whole Carpathian range, and on the highest peaks there is snow year-round. The whole region can suffer severe and unpleasant weather when bitterly cold, easterly winds blow from Russia. Between 1964 and 1993, the lowest recorded winter temperature in Bucharest was –26°F

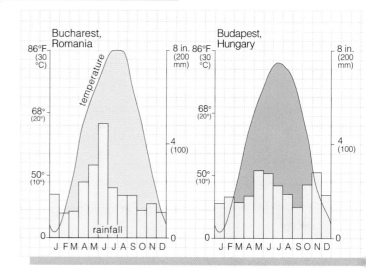

KEY FACTS

- In Hungary, spring and summer are the wettest times of the year. In early summer, almost 1 day in 3 may have a thunderstorm.
- Bucharest in July, with an average rainfall of 5 in (121 mm), is the rainiest spot in the region.

► **Golden Sands on the Black Sea was Bulgaria's first international resort. Summers here are like those in the east Mediterranean.**

(−32°C), in Warsaw 7°F (−14°C), and in Sofia −6°F (−21°C). Inland, the Danube and other rivers often freeze completely.

Winters tend to be a little warmer on the shores of the Black Sea in Romania and Bulgaria, with an average maximum between November and February of 43°F (6°C) in Constanta (Romania) and 46°F (8°C) in Varna (Bulgaria).

In the summer, the Czech Republic and Slovakia rarely experience extreme heat. Hungary's climate is affected by the position of various mountain ranges. For example, the Dinaric Alps block the moderating influence of the Atlantic Ocean. This gives the country a more extreme climate. Summer temperatures here can be high, with a maximum average between May and August of 77°F (25°C) in Debrecen. In Romania, the plains in the north and east can suffer from drought as hot, dry winds blow in from the Russian steppes. Bulgaria's climate is transitional between that of the Mediterranean and the continental type, with maximum inland summer temperatures averaging 82°F (28°C).

Throughout the region, rainfall tends to be moderate.

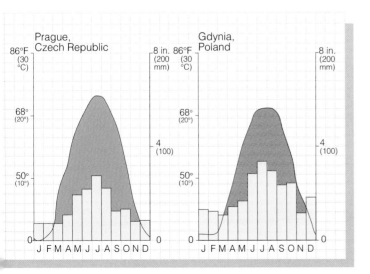

Eastern Europe has many important natural resources. Poland is Europe's largest, and the world's seventh largest, supplier of bituminous (hard) coal. Most of its estimated 65 million tons of reserves are in Upper Silesia. The country is also the world's fifth biggest supplier of brown coal and lignite (softer, but also more polluting, types of coal), with the Czech Republic sixth. By contrast, the combined coal reserves of Bulgaria, Hungary, Slovakia, and Romania amount to less than half of Poland's total.

Poland, Bulgaria, Hungary, and Romania also have reserves of natural gas. Poland's are estimated at about 157 billion cubic yards (121.4 billion m³). These cover about one-third of the country's demand for

▲ *Polish miners in Silesia. During the Communist period, the expression "Poland stands on coal" reflected the importance of coal for the country's wealth.*

▶ *A hydroelectric plant near Sopot, on the coast. Poland derives over 90% of its energy from coal-fired stations and the rest from hydroelectric stations.*

natural gas. Domestic production was 19,419 million cubic yards (4,949 million m³) in 1993, compared with Romania's figure of 83,644 million cubic yards (21,317 million m³)—more than four times as high.

Romania is the region's largest oil producer (6.7 million tons in 1994). It has seven offshore oil platforms in the Black Sea.

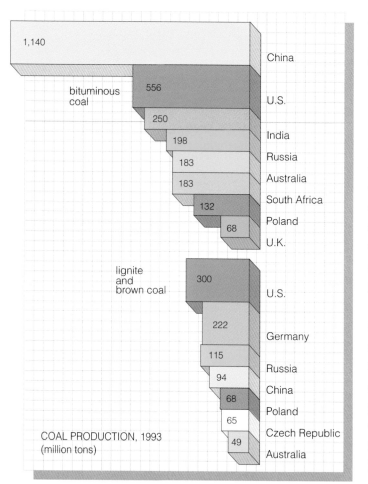

bituminous coal

1,140	China
556	U.S.
250	India
198	Russia
183	Australia
183	South Africa
132	Poland
68	U.K.

lignite and brown coal

300	U.S.
222	Germany
115	Russia
94	China
68	Poland
65	Czech Republic
49	Australia

COAL PRODUCTION, 1993
(million tons)

These account for more than 10 percent (%) of annual production of oil, gas, and coal. The second largest oil producer is Hungary (1.6 million tons in 1993). Bulgaria and Poland produce much smaller amounts, with Igaria's oil fields north of Varna on the Black Sea and inland near Pleven yielding only 43,000 tons in 1993. Although oil was discovered 50 miles (80 km) north of the port of Leba in 1985, Poland's oil reserves amount to an insignificant 100 million tons, with 158,000 tons of oil produced in 1992. By comparison, in 1992 the U.K. produced 100 million tons of oil and the U.S. 409 million.

With Greece and parts of former Yugoslavia, Hungary has the largest European reserves of bauxite, the principal ore in aluminum. Other minerals in the region include sulfur, of which Poland is Europe's second largest producer (19.3% in 1991); copper (Poland was the continent's third biggest producer in 1992, providing 12%); uranium (Czech Republic); iron ore and lead; manganese;

KEY FACTS

● Coal and coal products were Poland's second largest export item in 1994 (7.7% of the total).

● The oil fields in Romania's Carpathian and sub-Carpathian regions were once the largest in Europe, but these oil reserves are expected to be exhausted by the end of the 1990s.

● Production of bauxite in Hungary fell by 40% between 1991 and 1993, and then by another 40% between 1993 and 1994.

● The world's oldest uranium mine is in Jachymov in the Czech Republic.

zinc; and salt. Of the precious metals, gold is found in the Czech Republic, Bulgaria, and Hungary, and silver in Poland.

Sources of electricity vary throughout the region. Since Bulgaria has little oil, gas, or high-grade coal, in 1993 around 58% of its electricity was produced by low-grade coal-fired stations, 36% by nuclear power, and the rest by hydroelectricity. In Slovakia, the chief energy source for industry is

▼ **Kozlodui nuclear power plant in Bulgaria. According to the International Atomic Energy Agency, it contains two of Eastern Europe's six "unsafe" or "very dangerous" nuclear power reactors.**

hydroelectric power that is generated by a series of dams on several rivers, including the Vah River. There is also a dam on the Danube, at Gabcikovo. This began as a joint project in the late 1970s with Hungary, but Hungary withdrew from the project in 1992. More than 50% of Slovakia's electricity needs are provided by the nuclear power plant at Jaslovske-Bohunice. Hungary also relies heavily on nuclear power.

The first of six reactors in Romania's first nuclear power plant at Cernavoda came into operation in 1996. Poland has no nuclear power industry.

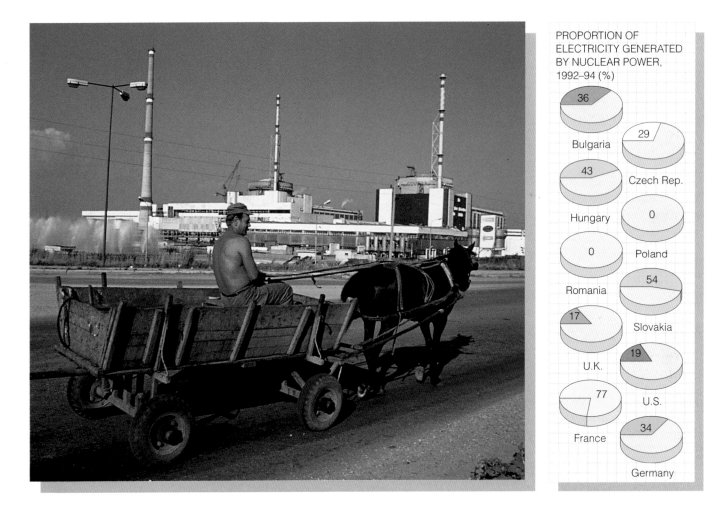

PROPORTION OF ELECTRICITY GENERATED BY NUCLEAR POWER, 1992–94 (%)

36 Bulgaria	29 Czech Rep.
43 Hungary	0 Poland
0 Romania	54 Slovakia
17 U.K.	19 U.S.
77 France	34 Germany

POPULATION

NUMBERS OF GYPSIES
(ROMANIES), 1990
(total and % of population)

Bulgaria
800,000 — 8.9%

Czech
Republic
and
Slovakia ★
800,000 — 5.1%

Hungary
600,000 — 6%

Romania
2,000,000 — 8.7%

Poland
50,000 — 0.13%

★ before the separation of Czechoslovakia

Population sizes in Eastern Europe vary considerably, from 38.6 million in Poland —40 percent (%) of the area's total—to 5.4 million in Slovakia (5.6%).

▲ *Gypsy girls in Romania. Eastern Europe's Gypsy population has increased by 35–40 percent since the mid-1970s. About half the world's Gypsies live in the region.*

ETHNIC GROUPS

In ethnic terms, the population of Poland is 98% Polish; that of Hungary 95% Hungarian; and that of the Czech Republic 96% Czech. Some of this uniformity is relatively recent. For example, in 1918, when the Czech lands and Slovakia came together to form Czechoslovakia, the new country had a rich multiethnic mix of Czechs, Jews, Ruthenians (who are of Ukrainian origin), Germans, Slovaks, and Hungarians. But most of the Jews were murdered by the Nazis during World War II. The eastern part of Slovakia where the Ruthenians lived was taken into the Soviet Union after that war. The Czechoslovak government expelled 2 million Germans after 1945. Slovaks and Hungarians left when Czechoslovakia split

into the Czech Republic and Slovakia on January 1, 1993.

There are significant ethnic minorities in Eastern Europe. The oldest and largest of these are the Gypsies (or Romanies), who have their historical roots in India and first came to southeastern Europe in the 13th century, or even earlier. In most countries, they suffer from discrimination.

In Sliven in Bulgaria, for instance, many of the 50,000 Gypsies who make up one-quarter of the city's population live in crowded and unsanitary conditions. It is common for three or four families to live in one home and for five or six people to sleep in the same room.

There are between 250,000 and 300,000 Poles of German origin, mostly in Silesia, which until 1919 was part of Germany and

▲ *Apartments at Banska Bystrica, Slovakia. As in the West, large, ugly housing projects sprang up rapidly in Eastern Europe after 1945.*

still has a somewhat German character. People here often speak both Polish and German and are loyal first to Silesia, not Poland.

The second largest minority in the region are the Hungarians in Romania (about 1.6 million, or 7% of the total population). There are also 600,000 Hungarians in Slovakia. These large minorities were created when the Austro-Hungarian Empire collapsed

URBAN POPULATION, 1995 (% of total population)

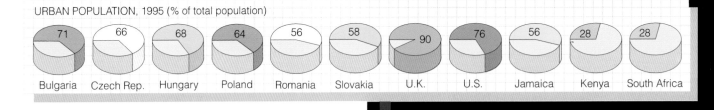

Bulgaria	Czech Rep.	Hungary	Poland	Romania	Slovakia	U.K.	U.S.	Jamaica	Kenya	South Africa
71	66	68	64	56	58	90	76	56	28	28

AGE STRUCTURE OF THE POPULATION, 1990 (% of total)

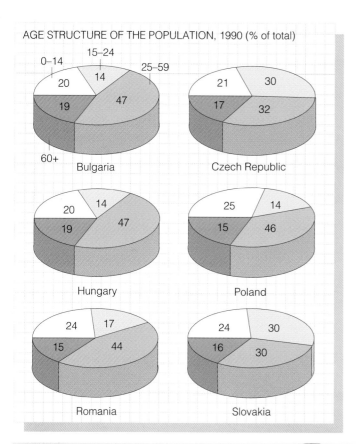

after World War I and a new, smaller Hungary was established that left many Hungarians living in neighboring countries. In both Romania and Slovakia, there are tensions between the governments and the Hungarian minorities. However, in March 1995, Slovakia and Hungary signed a treaty that guaranteed the rights of ethnic minorities in both countries.

URBANIZATION

In all East European countries, over half the population lives in urban areas. This is largely the result of the industrialization policies of Communist regimes in the 1950s and 1960s that drew people from the countryside to the cities. In Bulgaria, 26% of the population lived in towns and cities in 1950; in 1970 this figure had doubled to 52% and in 1995 it stood at 71%. In

◀ *Old peasant women in the village of Holloko in northern Hungary. This house, with its cellar at street level, its whitewashed walls, and its covered balcony, is typical of the area.*

◀ *Women working in the fields in Romania. The proportion of the workforce involved in agriculture fell from 75% in 1950 to 29% in 1993. Many of those living in rural areas, 44% of the total, are "rural commuters." They travel to towns and cities to work.*

▶ *Polish farmers transporting hay. Polish peasants cultivate small plots in the same way they have for centuries. From the air, Poland looks as if it has been cut into thousands of tiny strips. The cross in the photograph shows the central role of the Catholic Church in Polish life.*

Hungary, 61% of people live in the industrial north of the country. In the south and east, population density is only 37 people per square mile (60 per sq km), in contrast to the national average of 69 (111).

POPULATION GROWTH

Poland's population has had one of the highest rates of natural increase—a rise of 54% between 1950 and 1990, compared with the European average of 31%. But by the 1990s, the populations of most countries were growing slowly, or even declining, as a result of low birthrates. In Hungary, Poland, Romania, and Slovakia, an average of 37% of the population are less than 25 years old, while in the Czech Republic and Slovakia the average is 52.5%.

DAILY LIFE

The revolutions of 1989 and the removal of the Communist regimes have brought greater freedom and new prosperity for some people in the region, as well as insecurity. Newspapers and broadcasters are no longer subject to political control. People can speak as they wish in public, and travel abroad is not politically restricted. But unemployment is generally higher than in Western Europe and the U.S. The freedom to travel, for example, is available only to those who can afford it.

FAMILY LIFE

Under the Communist regimes, the family provided one of the few places where people could talk freely and relax. Today, the family still plays an important role in society, particularly in rural areas. Newly-weds often live with their parents or their in-laws. However, in towns and cities more and more young people are living away from their families, and an increasing (though still small) number of young couples are living together without getting married. In Poland, the number of

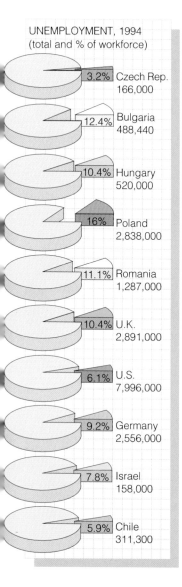

UNEMPLOYMENT, 1994
(total and % of workforce)

3.2% Czech Rep.
166,000

12.4% Bulgaria
488,440

10.4% Hungary
520,000

16% Poland
2,838,000

11.1% Romania
1,287,000

10.4% U.K.
2,891,000

6.1% U.S.
7,996,000

9.2% Germany
2,556,000

7.8% Israel
158,000

5.9% Chile
311,300

◄ *Miners and their families enjoying a picnic in Petrosan, Romania. A gas pipeline supplying their housing units runs behind them. The gap between the small, increasingly wealthy minority and the rest of the population—including these miners—is growing. The low living standards of the majority are reflected in the fact that in 1994, the average household spent 62 percent (%) of its income on food.*

EUROPEAN LANGUAGES

Indo-European family
- Germanic
- Roman
- Celtic
- Slavic
- Baltic
- Greek
- Albanian

Uralic family
- Finnish
- Hungarian

Altaic family
- Turkish

Basque family
- Basque

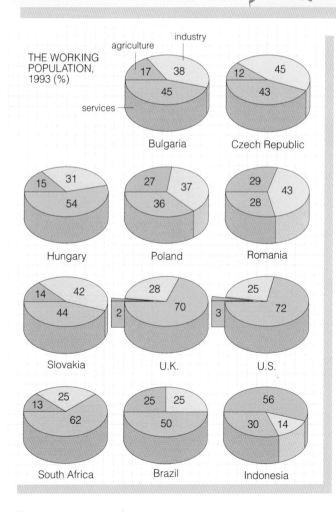

THE WORKING POPULATION, 1993 (%)

agriculture — industry — services

Bulgaria: 17 agriculture, 38 industry, 45 services

Czech Republic: 12, 45, 43

Hungary: 15, 31, 54

Poland: 27, 37, 36

Romania: 29, 43, 28

Slovakia: 14, 42, 44

U.K.: 2, 28, 70

U.S.: 3, 25, 72

South Africa: 13, 25, 62

Brazil: 25, 25, 50

Indonesia: 56, 30, 14

registered marriages is falling, from nine new marriages per 1,000 citizens a year, in 1980, to just over five in 1995. More children are also being born to parents who are not married. The figure has risen from 5 percent (%) of all babies born in 1976 to 9% of those born in 1995.

HEALTH

East Europeans enjoy free health care, although this service is under pressure because of underfunding and high demand.

NUMBERS OF TEACHERS AND STUDENTS IN HIGHER EDUCATION, 1993–94

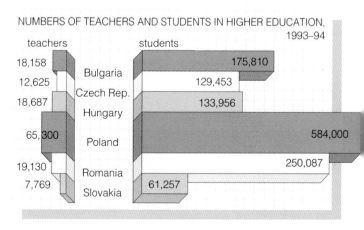

	teachers	students
Bulgaria	18,158	175,810
Czech Rep.	12,625	129,453
Hungary	18,687	133,956
Poland	65,300	584,000
Romania	19,130	250,087
Slovakia	7,769	61,257

KEY FACTS

● In 1990–95, Hungary and Romania had average infant mortality rates of 19 per 1,000 births, compared with 9 in the Czech Republic, 14 in Bulgaria, and 8 in the United States.

● Founded in 1348, Charles University in Prague is one of Europe's oldest universities.

● According to a World Economic Forum report of 1993, Bulgaria has an adult illiteracy rate of 8%, the highest in the Black Sea region.

● In 1989, the Roman Catholic Church in Poland was granted the right to operate its own schools. It now runs 900.

● In Hungary, there are 30,000 registered chess players who take part in competitions. Hungary is one of 6 countries whose players have won in the Chess Olympics, which have been held since 1927.

Poland and Romania provide the lowest level of health care in the region. Annual spending on health per head of population in Poland in 1995–96 was $67 and in Romania $49, compared with $1,100 in France and Germany. In Romania, there are 536 people per doctor and in Poland 451, compared with 311 in the Czech Republic and 320 in Germany. For the few people who can afford them, there are private medical services, too.

EDUCATION

Throughout the region, schooling is free and compulsory between the ages of 6 or 7 and 14 to 16, depending on the country. At secondary school level, pupils normally attend general or vocational schools that emphasize practical training. A greater proportion of young people attend higher education institutes than was the case under the Communists. In Hungary, the number of students in higher education rose by 50% between 1990 and 1993. It now includes about one in eight of all young people in the country. But the proportion of those in the region who are in higher education is still only about 25% of the U.S. average. In the U.S., about one in two young people enter higher education.

The education system has been undergoing great changes since 1989. Private and church-run schools have been established, for example, in Poland and Slovakia. Bilingual education is available for minorities, such as Germans and Hungarians in Romania, in spite of some continuing tensions with the majority populations and governments.

▼ *An elementary school mathematics class in Warsaw. Polish children begin school in the calendar year when they have their seventh birthday.*

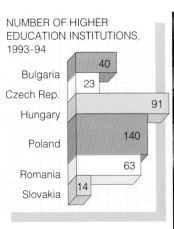

NUMBER OF HIGHER EDUCATION INSTITUTIONS, 1993–94

Bulgaria	40
Czech Rep.	23
Hungary	91
Poland	140
Romania	63
Slovakia	14

MAJOR EUROPEAN RELIGIONS

- Protestant
- Roman Catholic
- Greek and Russian Orthodox
- Islam

RELIGIONS

Most East Europeans are Christians, and the majority are Roman Catholics (94% of all Poles, 68% of Hungarians and 60% of Slovaks). In Bulgaria and Romania, most Christians belong to their country's Orthodox Church (83% of Romania's population, for example). Most of the region's 1.2 million Muslims live in Bulgaria. Newer Christian churches are also attracting followers. In Hungary, the evangelical movement known as "Faith" has about 100,000 members.

▼ *Rila Monastery, 75 miles (120 km) south of Sofia, Bulgaria. Founded in the 10th century, today Rila is both a center of worship and a tourist site.*

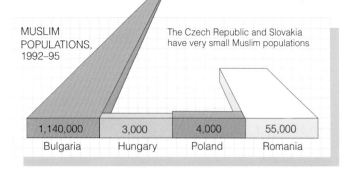

MUSLIM
POPULATIONS,
1992–95

The Czech Republic and Slovakia
have very small Muslim populations

Bulgaria	Hungary	Poland	Romania
1,140,000	3,000	4,000	55,000

▲ *The reopening of a mosque in Haskovo, Bulgaria. Muslims were discriminated against under the Communists, but their position today has improved.*

LEISURE

Sports and exercise are still not very popular in Eastern Europe. In late 1994, nine out of ten Poles questioned in a survey said that they played no regular sport and less than half exercised regularly. For those who did, soccer was the most popular sport, followed by volleyball and handball. Sports and fitness centers are beginning to appear, even though there are few of these, and they tend to be only in big cities.

The revolutions opened up Eastern Europe to many Western influences. Satellite dishes are springing up as people tune in to Western TV stations such as Sky and RTL. In February 1994, the U.S. company Central European Media Enterprises helped to start up Nova TV in the Czech Republic. This was Eastern Europe's first private national commercial television station. By January 1996, Nova had an average share of 70% of Czech TV viewers. Nova has the rights to show more than 6,000 foreign films and TV episodes.

MAJOR HOLIDAYS AND FESTIVALS

CHRISTIAN HOLIDAYS

March/April	EASTER (all countries)
May 6	ST. GEORGE'S DAY (Bulgaria)
July 5	INTRODUCTION OF CHRISTIANITY (Czech Republic and Slovakia)
August 15	ASSUMPTION OF THE VIRGIN MARY (Poland)
August 20	ST. STEPHEN'S DAY (Hungary)
December 25	CHRISTMAS DAY (all countries)

MUSLIM HOLIDAYS (Bulgaria)

February	SHEKER BAYRAM (Sugar Holiday), celebrating the end of the monthlong fast of Ramadan
April/May	KURBAN BAYRAM (Festival of the Sacrifice), celebrating Abraham's sacrifice of a sheep in place of his son

OTHER HOLIDAYS (all countries)

January 1	NEW YEAR'S DAY
May 1	LABOR DAY

▲ *Karel Poborsky (in white) scores the winning goal in the Czech Republic's 1–0 victory over Portugal in the quarterfinals of the Euro '96 soccer championships.*

RULES AND LAWS

Since the 1989 revolutions, free elections have been held in every Eastern European country, both for parliaments, or lawmaking bodies, and for heads of state.

The July 1989 elections in Poland were only partly free—65 percent of the seats in the parliament were reserved for the Communists. But when every contested seat except for one was won by the main opposition group, Solidarity, the end of the unpopular Communist regime was in sight. The first fully free elections in Poland, Hungary, and Czechoslovakia (1990–91) also produced victories for political parties that had been associated with the DISSIDENT opposition to communism before 1989. The new presidents of these countries had also been critics of the old system. Poland's Lech Walesa (woe-when-sah) had become famous in the 1980s as the leader of the Solidarity movement and, like President Vaclav Havel in Czechoslovakia, he had served time in jail under the Communists.

By the mid-1990s, however, former Communists had been returned to power in most East European countries. For instance, the Hungarian Socialist Party (the renamed Communist party), formed a government in May 1995 with the Alliance of Free

Democrats, many of whose leading members are former dissidents. In Poland, the September 1993 election produced an overwhelming victory for parties dominated by former Communists and their allies. In 1996, the ex-Communist Alexander Kwasniewski succeeded Lech Walesa as president. In Bulgaria, where there was no strong anti-Communist opposition before

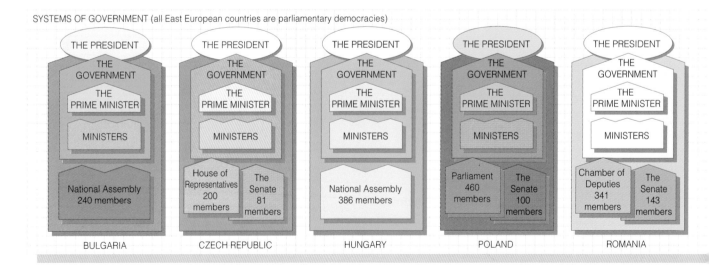

SYSTEMS OF GOVERNMENT (all East European countries are parliamentary democracies)

THE PRESIDENT	THE PRESIDENT	THE PRESIDENT	THE PRESIDENT	THE PRESIDENT
THE GOVERNMENT	THE GOVERNMENT	THE GOVERNMENT	THE GOVERNMENT	THE GOVERNMENT
THE PRIME MINISTER	THE PRIME MINISTER	THE PRIME MINISTER	THE PRIME MINISTER	THE PRIME MINISTER
MINISTERS	MINISTERS	MINISTERS	MINISTERS	MINISTERS
National Assembly 240 members	House of Representatives 200 members / The Senate 81 members	National Assembly 386 members	Parliament 460 members / The Senate 100 members	Chamber of Deputies 341 members / The Senate 143 members
BULGARIA	CZECH REPUBLIC	HUNGARY	POLAND	ROMANIA

▲ *November 24, 1989, 300,000 Czechoslovak citizens crowd into Wenceslas Square in central Prague to demonstrate their opposition to the Communist regime. The largely peaceful nature of this revolution earned it the title of the "Velvet Revolution."*

1989, renamed and reformed Communists have since been voted into power. By contrast, in the Czech Republic conservative political parties have been in government since the second free elections in 1992.

In some countries, the turnout at elections has been low, sometimes close to 50%. These low figures, together with the votes for former Communists (and other left-wing parties), indicate that some people are unhappy with the consequences of the new economic reforms, or that they think politicians are unable to solve economic problems. For example, in Romania since 1990 there have been many, sometimes violent, demonstrations against price increases, low wages, and unemployment.

Economic insecurity is one factor behind an increase in crime. In the Czech Republic, the murder rate has quadrupled since 1989. However, crime rates are still lower than in Western European countries and the U.S.

Frustration with the new system has also encouraged old prejudices, and there is increased discrimination against ethnic and religious minorities. It is the Gypsies who are the main targets of the new racism. In 1991, there were organized attacks on these communities throughout Romania,

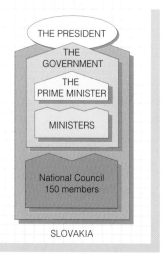

THE PRESIDENT

THE GOVERNMENT

THE PRIME MINISTER

MINISTERS

National Council
150 members

SLOVAKIA

KEY FACTS

● After his abdication in 1947, King Mihai of Romania worked as a farmer growing vegetables in England, then as a test pilot and broker in Switzerland.
● In Bulgaria, the Muslim minority has its own political party—the Movement for Rights and Freedom. In the December 1994 elections, it won 15 seats in the National Assembly.
● Between 1988 and 1995, the proportion of women in national parliaments fell from 29.3% to 10% in Hungary; from 23% to 13% in Poland; and from 34% to 3% in Romania.

leading many Gypsies to emigrate to Germany. In 1992–94, Germany sent about 25,000 of them back, even though physical attacks on Gypsies in Romania were increasing.

Nationalism was an important force in the 1989 revolutions. Ordinary citizens felt they were freeing their countries from Communist regimes that were "foreign" because they were backed by the Soviet Union. Today, nationalism is still strong. The most important such development since 1989 has been the Slovak push for independence. On January 1, 1993, this ended in the disappearance of Czechoslovakia and the emergence of the Czech Republic and Slovakia.

In Romania, some people would like the monarchy back. King Mihai was forced out

▲ *A Bulgarian voting in June 1990. This election brought former Communists to power, but in December 1990 they were toppled by strikes and demonstrations.*

PEOPLE WISHING TO RETURN TO COMMUNIST RULE (%)
responses to opinion poll, early 1996

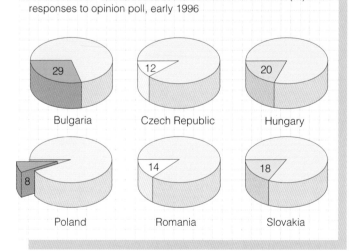

Bulgaria	Czech Republic	Hungary
29	12	20

Poland	Romania	Slovakia
8	14	18

◀ *Tadeusz Mazowiecki, a former dissident, became Poland's prime minister in August 1989. He was the region's first non-Communist prime minister since the 1940s.*

▼ *Soldiers in Iasi, Romania. Military service is compulsory in the region and lasts from 12 to 18 months, depending on the country.*

by the Communists in 1947. Since 1989, he has tried to return to the country several times, but the government, afraid of his popularity, has refused to let him in.

Despite the hardships that many people in Eastern Europe face, there is no indication that a majority want to return to communism. In early 1996, only an average of 17% in the region said that they wanted the old system back.

FOOD AND FARMING

Agriculture in Eastern Europe has under-gone considerable change in the last few years. Before 1989, most farms were either COOPERATIVES or owned by the state. (The exception was Poland, where three-quarters of arable land were privately owned.)

Since 1989, much agricultural land has been privatized. In Bulgaria, private farming was legalized in 1990, and by 1994 privately owned farms supplied 72 percent (%) of produce. In the Czech Republic, the figure was 90%, with private farms accounting for 85% of all arable land. One principal method of privatization has been returning land that was once confiscated by Communist governments to its former owners.

Government allowances to farmers have been cut—in Hungary by 50% in 1991; in Poland by almost 100%. At the same time, farmers have been able to sell less at home because people are poorer as a result of the economic reforms. In 1994 in the Czech Republic, farms had an overall loss of US$76 million because of the decline in purchases of food. Farmers are also no longer guaranteed sales in other Communist countries. Also the European Union only imports a limited amount of farm products from Eastern Europe, less than 1% of European Union consumption.

As a result, agricultural production levels have dropped. In Bulgaria, total crop production fell from 9.65 million tons to 5.44 million between 1989 and 1993. In Slovakia, the fall was from 11.05 million to 8.23 million. Many farmworkers have become unemployed. In the Czech Republic the agricultural labor force shrank by 40% between 1990 and 1994.

If East European agriculture is to compete internationally, it will have to become more efficient, raising production levels without increasing employment. In the European Union, only about one person in 20 makes a living from the land. In the U.S., 17% of the workforce are employed in

◄ *Farmers plowing a field in Poland. Like Hungary, Poland is a large exporter of food. But since the change to a market economy, it now imports more than it exports. This is because its food industry does not provide the quality that Poles now expect.*

► *An open market in Sandanski, Bulgaria. With 110 cloudless days and 2,500 hours of sunshine a year, Sandanski is famous for its abundant fruit and vegetables. About 6% of Bulgaria's agricultural land is planted with produce such as potatoes, melons, and berries. In the early 1990s, exporting fresh produce to Western Europe was made very difficult by the crisis in former Yugoslavia.*

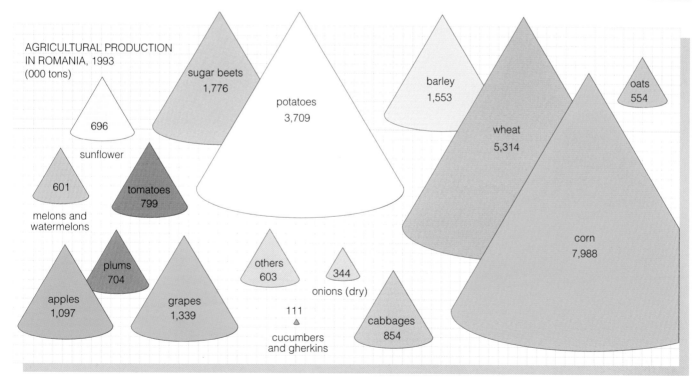

AGRICULTURAL PRODUCTION IN ROMANIA, 1993 (000 tons)

sugar beets 1,776

potatoes 3,709

barley 1,553

oats 554

696

sunflower

wheat 5,314

601

melons and watermelons

tomatoes 799

plums 704

others 603

344

onions (dry)

corn 7,988

apples 1,097

grapes 1,339

111

cucumbers and gherkins

cabbages 854

◀ *Dried paprika on sale at an indoor market in Budapest. This is one of Hungary's best-known agricultural products.*

▼ *A Budapest meat stand selling sausages. There are many types of spicy sausages popular with both Hungarians and tourists.*

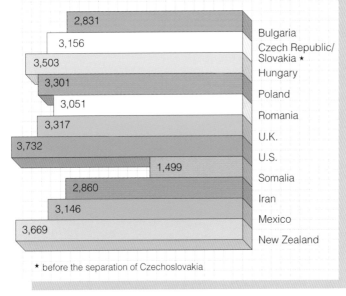

FOOD SUPPLY, 1992 (calories per person per day)

	Calories	Country
	2,831	Bulgaria
	3,156	Czech Republic/Slovakia ★
	3,503	Hungary
	3,301	Poland
	3,051	Romania
	3,317	U.K.
	3,732	U.S.
	1,499	Somalia
	2,860	Iran
	3,146	Mexico
	3,669	New Zealand

★ before the separation of Czechoslovakia

agriculture, and they produce 2% of GROSS DOMESTIC PRODUCT (GDP), the total goods and services. But in Poland, the figures are almost 26% (about 3.7 million people) who produce 7% of the GDP.

Despite its grimy, industrial image, Eastern Europe is very rural. About 58% of its land area is used for agriculture, compared with 43% for the European Union. Agriculture accounts for an average of 10% of GDP, compared with about 2.5% in the European Union. Around 75% of farmland is used for growing crops. The principal types are cereals (wheat, corn, barley), potatoes, and sugar beets.

The Czech Republic is famous for its

KEY FACTS

● The average size of a Polish farm is 17 acres (7 ha) (compared with a European Union average of 40 acres [16 ha]).

● In Romania, the privatization of agriculture has become bogged down in legal arguments. At the beginning of 1996, there were more than 1 million unresolved court cases involving land disputes.

● In 1993, Romania was the world's 9th largest producer of wine (800,000 tons), Hungary the 14th, Bulgaria the 20th, Slovakia the 28th, and the Czech Republic the 34th. Top of the list was Italy (5.7 million tons), followed by France and Spain.

● In 1993, Poland was the world's 2nd largest producer of potatoes (36,271,000 tons), after Russia (38,000,000 tons).

hops. Known as "green gold," they give Czech beer its distinctive flavor and help make this one of the country's major products and exports.

About 25% of farmland is used for raising livestock: primarily pigs, poultry, cattle, and sheep. Romania is Eastern Europe's largest producer of lamb and has three-fifths of the region's sheep. In Poland, poultry, pigs, and cattle are the main livestock. In 1993, meat and dairy products accounted for 62% of the country's total agricultural production and 3.2% of its export income. Processed foods are also important exports. They include jams and gherkins from Bulgaria, and beets from Poland.

Meat and dumplings are typical dishes in Eastern Europe. A traditional Czech meal is pork, dumplings, and cabbage, and Poland is famous for bigos, a casserole of sauerkraut, beef, and pork. In Slovakia, thick soups known as zapraska are made with cabbage, potato, beans, and mushrooms. Food in Bulgaria shows signs of Turkish influence, with kabobs and grilled meatballs part of the staple diet. Since the revolutions, Western fast foods, such as those available at McDonald's restaurants, have become increasingly popular.

People's diets are slowly changing. This is partly because economic reforms have made meat more expensive and healthful foods, such as fruit and vegetables, cheaper. In Poland, advertising has contributed to the popularity of items such as margarine that were almost unknown until 1990.

◀ *A rose picker near Kazanluk in the Valley of the Roses, Bulgaria. Bulgaria earns US$30 million a year supplying 70% of the world's rose extract (attar) for the cosmetics industry. Bulgarians call roses "Bulgaria's gold." 2,000 rose petals are required for .04 of an ounce (1 g) of attar.*

TRADE AND INDUSTRY

◀ *Women bottling gherkins in Kazanluk, Bulgaria. Food and agricultural products are Bulgaria's single largest export category.*

EXPORTS AND OVERSEAS LINKS

The recovery in the "fast-track" states has been driven by exports, especially to Germany and elsewhere in the European Union (55–65% of the total in 1994). In 1994, their total volume of exports increased by 11.5%. Exports are important because they earn the money needed to pay for the modernization of factories and mines and for the construction of road and rail links.

Romania, and Bulgaria even more, will benefit from the new importance of the Black Sea as a trade route linking them with the former Soviet Union and oil-rich areas in the Caspian Sea, Central Asia, and the Middle East. Russia, Bulgaria, and Greece plan to build

ECONOMIC CHANGES

Since 1989, all the countries have begun to introduce Western-style market economies. The first and biggest changes came in Poland, Czechoslovakia, and Hungary, the "fast-track" states. The government's role in managing the economy was reduced, and the countries were opened up to competition with the rest of the world, including Western Europe, North America, and the Far East. As a result, many government employees were let go, some unproductive factories closed, and overall production fell. In 1994, average industrial production in Eastern Europe was only 64 percent (%) of the 1989 level. Unemployment also rose. In Poland, the figure stood at 1.13 million (6.3% of the workforce) in 1990. A year later, it was 2.16 million (11.8%). However, by the mid-1990s, prospects for these countries seemed to be brighter. Although unemployment was still high, it was beginning to drop or had stabilized. The economies were growing by up to 5% each year.

By contrast, in Romania and Bulgaria, where reforms were introduced later and gradually, economic growth was slower.

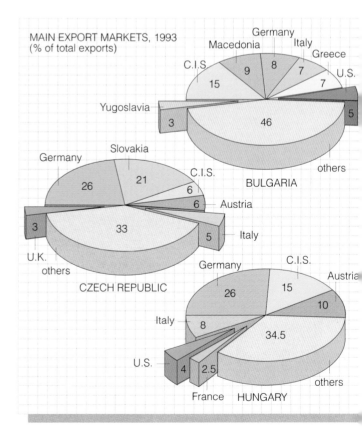

MAIN EXPORT MARKETS, 1993
(% of total exports)

BULGARIA: Germany, Macedonia 9, Italy 8, Greece 7, U.S. 7, C.I.S. 15, Yugoslavia 3, others 46, 5

CZECH REPUBLIC: Germany 26, Slovakia 21, C.I.S. 6, Austria 6, Italy 5, U.K. 3, others 33

HUNGARY: Germany 26, C.I.S. 15, Austria 10, others 34.5, Italy 8, U.S. 4, France 2.5

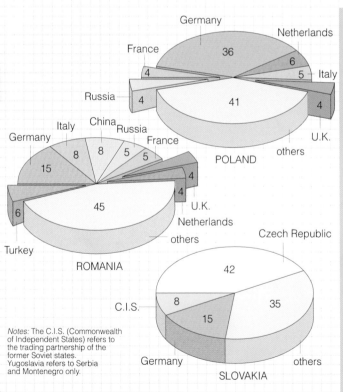

Germany
France
36
Netherlands
6
4
5 — Italy
Russia
4
41
4
China Russia
Italy
France
U.K.
Germany
8
8
5
5
others
15
POLAND
4
4
45
U.K.
6
Netherlands
others
Turkey
ROMANIA
Czech Republic
42
C.I.S.
8
35
15
Germany
others
SLOVAKIA

Notes: The C.I.S. (Commonwealth of Independent States) refers to the trading partnership of the former Soviet states. Yugoslavia refers to Serbia and Montenegro only.

▲ *A steelworks in Sofia. In 1992, Bulgaria exported 350,000 tons of iron and steel products. But imports of iron ore are higher: 723,000 tons in 1994.*

a 217-mile (350-km) pipeline to transport more than 40 million tons of Russian oil a year from the port of Burgas in Bulgaria to Alexandroupolis in Greece.

Foreign companies have invested in Eastern Europe, for example, in the form of JOINT VENTURES and new businesses. It is cheaper for them to operate in Eastern than in Western Europe. For instance, the Italian firm Fiat makes its small Cinquecento car, which is sold throughout Europe, in Poland.

For Eastern Europe, investment is good because it brings modern technology and creates access to foreign markets.

The Skoda Octavia. Skoda, the Czech Republic's leading car company, was founded in 1895. In 1991, it became part of Germany's Volkswagen group.

STRUCTURE OF GDP, 1993 (%)

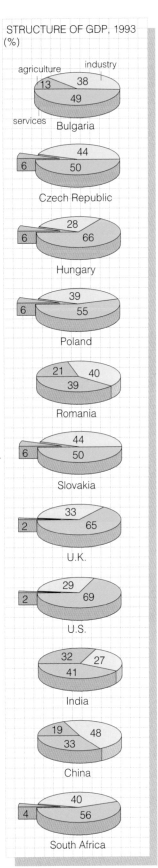

agriculture — industry

13 / 38 / 49
services — Bulgaria

44 / 6 / 50
Czech Republic

28 / 6 / 66
Hungary

39 / 6 / 55
Poland

21 / 40 / 39
Romania

44 / 6 / 50
Slovakia

33 / 2 / 65
U.K.

29 / 2 / 69
U.S.

32 / 27 / 41
India

19 / 48 / 33
China

40 / 4 / 56
South Africa

Glass blowing in northern Bohemia in the Czech Republic dates back to the 11th century. In 1995, the foreign sales of the 120 top glass manufacturers were US$135 million, up by 8.9% over 1994.

MAJOR INDUSTRIES

The average size of the industrial sector was 39% in 1993 (compared with 33% in Great Britain and 29% in the U.S.). The region produces and exports everything from raw materials (Polish coal) to specialized foods (paprika and honey from Hungary). Bulgaria's main products range from cement and pig iron to cigarettes and cotton fabrics; Hungary's vary from steel to textiles and clothing, electronic goods, and railroad coaches. The Czech Republic is noted for its precision instruments (such as medical and dental equipment, and

KEY FACTS

● Production of the most famous Czech beer, Budweiser, has doubled since 1991—from 13 million to 26 million gallons (500,000 to 1 million hl) a year.

● About 15% of Poland's exports consist of goods and services sold to "tourists" within 62 mi (100 km) of the frontier. About 63% of this trade is on the German border.

● The first World Dracula Congress took place in Romania in May 1995. For a few hundred dollars, Dracula fans from the West were taken on a 5-day tour of Transylvania – the home of Vlad the Impaler, the medieval prince on whom Dracula is based.

● The Slovak Air Force charges tourists US$8,000 for a 4-day course where they are passengers in a MiG-21 "Fulcrum" jet.

▼ *Rug weaving on a handloom in Romania. Other peasant crafts there include making ceramics and carving intricate decorations for buildings and on furniture.*

electronic components for cars), and for its engineering industry. Poland's shipbuilding industry is a major source of the country's export earnings. It is the world's fifth largest producer of merchant vessels.

Smaller-scale and cottage industries in the region include glass blowing, lace, and wood carving in the Czech Republic, and porcelain and textiles in Hungary.

TOURISM

Tourism is increasingly important in some countries. In Hungary, earnings from Western tourism in 1993 came to nearly US$1.2 billion, up from $267 million in 1985. The most popular destinations are Prague, Budapest, the Carpathian Mountains, and the Black Sea shores of Bulgaria and Romania. In 1989, 23 million foreigners visited the Czech lands; while in 1995, the Czech Republic had 98 million visitors, 45% of whom visited Prague.

TRANSPORTATION

During the Communist era, Eastern Europe's transportation systems suffered from lack of investment. In Poland, for example, the main east–west road linking Warsaw with Berlin in Germany and Moscow in Russia still has only two lanes. The country now has plans to build 1,615 miles (2,600 km) of highways by the year 2010. These will link with roads coming into the country from the Czech Republic, Slovakia, Austria, Germany, Belarus, Ukraine, and Russia. In Romania, a major project to improve 621 miles (1,000 km) of highways and modernize border crossings was begun in 1993.

Throughout the region, trains and buses are cheap and popular forms of travel. In 1994, the British-based National Express rail company, in cooperation with local transportation firms, began running services that connect Warsaw with 17 other cities, including Krakow and Gdansk. All the region's capitals, and some other major cities, have streetcar systems.

Since the collapse of communism, the demand for passenger vehicles has greatly

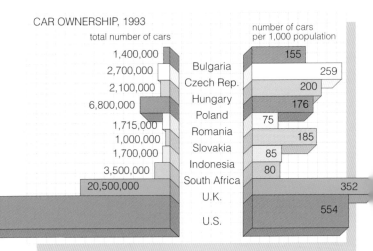

CAR OWNERSHIP, 1993

	total number of cars		number of cars per 1,000 population
Bulgaria	1,400,000		155
Czech Rep.	2,700,000		259
Hungary	2,100,000		200
Poland	6,800,000		176
Romania	1,715,000		75
Slovakia	1,000,000		185
Indonesia	1,700,000		85
South Africa	3,500,000		80
U.K.	20,500,000		352
U.S.	146,300,000		554

◀ **The Chain Bridge is the oldest of the 7 bridges that span the Danube to link Buda and Pest, the 2 halves of Hungary's capital. It was opened in 1849.**

▶ **In Prague, a streetcar travels the narrow streets in the Lesser Quarter beneath Castle Hill. Throughout the region, the streetcar offers cheap urban transportation.**

increased. Between 1989 and 1993, the number of privately owned cars rose by 19 percent (%) in Bulgaria, by 21% in Hungary, and by 40% in Poland, compared with increases of 4% in Great Britain and 2.5% in the U.S. In Bulgaria, where many vehicles are secondhand, the average age of a car is 15–17 years.

The Hungarian transportation system is largely based around Budapest. All main routes radiate outward from the capital, with the result that traffic in the city is heavily congested. To the south of Budapest, there are only two bridges for vehicles across the Danube, and one for trains, which makes east–west travel very difficult.

Freight is carried mainly by trucks and railroads. This, combined with economic growth, has produced a surge in sales of heavy trucks (those weighing more than 16 tons) to Eastern Europe. In 1995, sales of imported commercial vehicles in Poland rose by 57% compared with 1994 (to 3,504). It is predicted that annual sales of heavy trucks in the region will average up to 52,000 over the next 20 years.

Rivers and canals are also used to transport freight. The main shipping route is the Danube. The Danube–Rhine–Main canal in Germany makes the river part of a continuous system of transportation that stretches from the North Sea to the Black Sea. The chief port on the Black Sea is Constanta in Romania. Romania and Bulgaria are both part of the 11-member Black Sea Economic Cooperation group. This was set up in 1994, and its priority is cooperation in the energy sector. On Poland's coast, Gdansk has been an important trading center for 700 years.

KEY FACTS

● In 1993, the total road network in Eastern Europe was 268,101 mi (431,456 km) long, compared with 237,370 mi (382,000 km) in the U.K. alone.
● Romania's rate of car ownership (75 per 1,000 inhabitants) is the second lowest in Europe (after Albania).
● Continental Europe's first underground railroad was built in Budapest in 1896. Poland's first stretch of underground, 7 mi (11.25 km) long, opened in Warsaw in April 1995.
● Between 1949 and 1953, the construction of the Danube–Black Sea Canal in Romania cost the lives of more than 100,000 workers. It was known as the Canal of Death.
● Registered in 1923, Czech Airlines is the oldest airline in Europe.

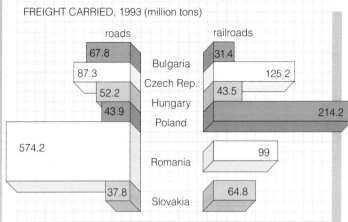

FREIGHT CARRIED, 1993 (million tons)

	roads	railroads
Bulgaria	67.8	31.4
Czech Rep.	87.3	125.2
Hungary	52.2	43.5
Poland	43.9	214.2
Romania	574.2	99
Slovakia	37.8	64.8

▲ **The port of Constanta. The collapse of communism in Eastern Europe in 1989 ended Soviet influence over ports such as this.**

The Danube is also a favorite travel route for tourists, who can travel by hydrofoil from Vienna in Austria to Bratislava in Slovakia or Budapest in Hungary.

Most tourists travel to Eastern Europe by car or train. Between January and September 1995, 71 million people (96.3% of the total) traveled to the Czech Republic by car or bus, 1.7 million (2.4%) by rail and 959,400 (1.3%) by plane. There are also domestic air services in all Eastern European countries.

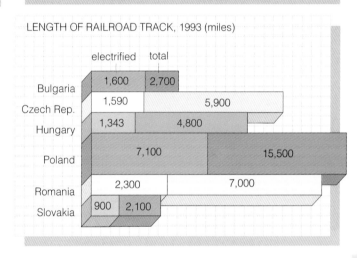

LENGTH OF RAILROAD TRACK, 1993 (miles)

	electrified	total
Bulgaria	1,600	2,700
Czech Rep.	1,590	5,900
Hungary	1,343	4,800
Poland	7,100	15,500
Romania	2,300	7,000
Slovakia	900	2,100

▼ **A barge carrying freight on the Danube in Slovakia. Throughout European history, the river has been an important route for trade and migration.**

THE ENVIRONMENT

Anger at the destruction of the environment and the dangerously high levels of pollution was one reason that people challenged the Communist regimes.

The pollution was caused by several factors. Power stations used low-grade fuels, such as brown (soft) coal that produces high levels of sulfur dioxide, the principal cause of acid rain. Exhaust fumes from public and private vehicles were not controlled. And large-scale industrial complexes were built without proper filtration and purification plants. The effects of these pollutants will be felt for many years.

The worst affected area is the curve that includes southeastern Germany (formerly southern East Germany, which was also in the Communist bloc), the northwestern part of the Czech Republic, southern Poland, and eastern Slovakia. Brown coal is the major culprit. For example, 75 percent (%) of the Czech Republic's electricity is produced by power stations that burn this fuel. With a population of 10.4 million, the Czech Republic produces 5 tons of sulfur dioxide per square mile (13 per sq km), about twice as much as the western part of Germany produces with a population of around 60 million.

More than half of Poland's 800 towns and cities have no sewage or wastewater

▶ *Children playing in polluted water at Copsa Mica, Romania. Lead poisoning is widespread there. In 1995, it was identified as 1 of 24 areas in the country with intense pollution problems.*

KEY FACTS

● Nearly 3 million Poles in Upper Silesia live with up to 390 tons of dust per sq mi (1,000 per sq km)—4 times the maximum permitted level.

● 35–40% of Hungary's population lives with officially unacceptable air and water pollution. Air pollution will cost Hungary US$374 million in 1992–97 because of illness and premature death.

● The Carpathian Mountains in Romania are home to many wild animals: the marmot (a woodchuck or groundhog), the chamois (a wild antelope), wild boars, the mountain lynx, the brown bear, and wolves.

● Europe's largest bird sanctuary opened in April 1994. Covering 55 sq mi (142 sq km), it straddles the border between Austria and Hungary, in the area around Neusiedler Lake

purification plants, and all waste flows untreated into the sea. The treatment plants that exist are mostly ineffective.

Since 1990, there have been some improvements. In Bulgaria, the use of fertilizers fell from a high of 165 pounds (185 kg) per acre (ha) in 1985 to 40 pounds (45 kg) in 1994, and the use of pesticides fell from 69 pounds (76.5 kg) in 1985 to 14.2 pounds (16.1 kg) in 1992. This reduction is partly due to the shrinking of the agricultural sector.

Some governments have been taking steps to combat pollution. Slovakia has introduced most of the European Union's 200 environmental directives, or guides. These cover matters such as stipulating the levels of lead in gas and limiting sulfur dioxide emissions from power plants. But these measures are expensive. The Romanian government has approved 102 environmental projects for 1996–99, which will cost US$500 million. Romania needs

◄ *A waste dump in Usti nad Labem, near the Czech border with Germany and Poland. Dumping waste is a problem throughout the region. In the early 1990s, two-thirds of the 30 million tons of hazardous waste that Poland generates each year were dumped in unregulated sites.*

◀ *Trees on the Polish-Czech border killed by acid rain. About 26% of Czech forests have been destroyed or damaged since 1945.*

foreign funding to cover 40% of the cost.

Environmental groups play an important role in some countries. In Poland, the Polish Ecology Club, which is highly praised for its scientific expertise, is very active. There are also many local organizations, such as the Ecology Club run by the Franciscan monks.

Eastern Europe has many nature preserves and conservation areas, rich in biological resources. Access to parts or all of these areas is limited. In 1987, 9.2% of Poland consisted of protected areas; the target for the year 2000 is 15%. In Romania, the Danube Delta is home to more than 300 species of birds and 1,150 kinds of plants. Hungary is famous for its thermal waters, whose high mineral content has led to the development of health spas.

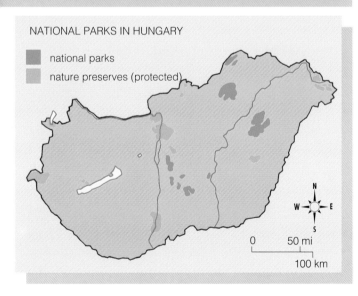

NATIONAL PARKS IN HUNGARY

■ national parks
■ nature preserves (protected)

0   50 mi
100 km

N
W—E
S

▶ **One of the 250 European bison in a preserve in Bialowezia Forest, Poland— the last fragment of the ancient forest that once covered the whole of Europe.**

THE FUTURE

After the euphoria of the revolutions of 1989 and the collapse of communism, the countries of Eastern Europe are faced with a number of challenges. High unemployment, ethnic and nationalist tensions, rising crime levels, and economic insecurity all threaten to weaken popular support for the market economy and parliamentary democracy.

Eastern European governments must develop roads, railroads, telecommunications systems, stock exchanges, banks, airports, and power stations if their countries are to compete effectively with those in the rest of the world. For example, in 1993 Romania had only 11,600 telephone lines per 1,000 inhabitants (20% of the European average). With help from the World Bank and the European Bank for Reconstruction and Development, it has embarked on a program to install 500,000 lines. Investment in the region from overseas is vital for its development. In 1995, such investment rose to US$4.4 billion in Hungary (compared with $1.15 billion in 1993), and to $2.5 billion in the Czech Republic (from $878 million in 1994).

Western governments have an important role to play in encouraging prosperity and democracy in the region. All East European countries have applied for membership in the European Union. They argue that this would strengthen the process of economic and political reform at home. But by September 1996, the Union had not yet set a date for entry negotiations to begin.

East European states also want to join NATO, the Western military alliance. They say that this would make them more secure in the face of instability in Russia and other former Soviet states. So far (1996), NATO has only granted them membership, together with former Soviet states and others, in a loose group known as "Partnership for Peace."

Eastern Europe is undergoing a unique period of change. Despite the uncertainties, the signs are that the economic and political reforms in the region will succeed.

KEY FACTS

● In 1990–95, Hungary, Poland, the Czech Republic, and Slovakia accounted for more than two-thirds of foreign investment in Eastern Europe.

● Daewoo, the South Korean car firm, controls 3 vehicle manufacturers in the region: Automobile Craiova in Romania, Avia in the Czech Republic, and FS Lublin in Poland.

● In January 1996, Hungary opened its first toll road, a highway linking Budapest with Vienna in Austria.

▲ *Volkswagen was one of the first big Western companies to set up in Eastern Europe. Its plant in Bratislava, Slovakia, is part-owned by a local company, Bratislavske Automobilove Zavody.*

▶ *The East-West Business Center, Budapest. About 40–45% of foreign investment in Hungary is from the U.S. There are more than 400 U.S. businesses in the country.*

FURTHER INFORMATION

● EMBASSY OF THE REPUBLIC OF BULGARIA
1621 22nd Street, N.W.
Washington, D.C. 20008

● EMBASSY OF CZECH REPUBLIC
3900 Spring of Freedom Street, N.W.
Washington, D.C. 20008

● EMBASSY OF THE REPUBLIC OF HUNGARY
3910 Shoemaker Street, N.W.
Washington, D.C. 20008

● EMBASSY OF POLAND
2640 16th Street, N.W.
Washington, D.C. 20009

● EMBASSY OF ROMANIA
1607 23rd Street, N.W.
Washington, D.C. 20008

● EMBASSY OF THE SLOVAK REPUBLIC
2201 Wisconsin Avenue, N.W., Suite 250
Washngton, D.C. 20007

More detailed information about Eastern Europe can be found in various sources in public libraries. Please check sources like the Statesman's Year Book*, which is published annually; the* Europa Year Book*; Worldmark Encyclopedia of the Nations; and* Peoples of the World, Eastern Europe and the Post-Soviet Republic.

BOOKS ABOUT EASTERN EUROPE

Bulgaria in Pictures. Lerner, 1994
Hintz, Martin. *Hungary*. Childrens, 1988
Holland, Gini. *Poland*. Gareth Stevens, 1992
Popescu, Julian. *Bulgaria*. Chelsea House, 1988
Popescu, Julian. *Hungary*. Chelsea House, 1988
Stewart, Gail B. *Romania*. Macmillan, 1991
Symynkywicz, Jeffrey. *Vaclav Havel and the Velvet Revolution*. Macmillan, 1995

GLOSSARY

COMMUNISM
An economic and political system in which the state controls most of the economy and private ownership is largely abolished.

COOPERATIVE
An association of peasants who have pooled (or been forced to pool) their land and resources for the purposes of joint cultivation.

DELTA
The triangular-shaped area at the mouth of a river where the river divides into many small branches flowing into the sea.

DEMOCRACY
A country that is ruled by the politicians elected by the people of that country.

DISSIDENT
Someone who is strongly and outspokenly opposed to the policies of a government or political party.

GROSS DOMESTIC PRODUCT
The total value of all the goods and services produced by a country in a year, except for investments abroad.

HOLOCAUST
The murder of six million Jews during the Second World War by the Nazi regime in Germany.

JOINT VENTURE
The setting up of a new firm by two or more private or public enterprises, for the purpose of carrying out a particular project.

MARKET ECONOMY
The economic system in which all or most businesses are owned privately, and the government does not intervene to influence supply or demand. For example, the government does not state what items should be produced, or control prices.

INDEX